KAIRY M. SPRINGER

A Needle in a Haystack

More than stories of lost love- this is a testimony of resilience, faith, and the priceless gift of choosing yourself.

First edition November 2025

ISBN 978-1-2570-2512-1 (paperback)

To my daughters,

You are the heartbeat of this book. Your laughter, your questions, your strength, and even your silence have shaped me. Watching you grow has been both a mirror and a compass—reflecting my journey and guiding me toward healing. These pages are my gift to you, not just as your mother, but as a woman who has stumbled, prayed, and risen. I want you to know: no mistake defines you, no heartbreak disqualifies you, and no detour is wasted when God holds the map.

With Love,

Mom

⊚ *Table of Content*

A Needle in a Haystack

Foreword

When I read my mom's words, I don't just see a story I see her. The woman who taught me strength without ever having to say the word. The woman who laughed through pain, prayed through storms, and somehow always managed to lift others while rebuilding herself.

This book, *A Needle in a Haystack*, isn't just about relationships or heartbreaks it's about rediscovery. It's about faith, forgiveness, and the beauty that can still grow from broken ground. My mom doesn't write from a place of bitterness. She writes from healing. From lessons learned the hard way and grace that can only come from God.

What makes this book powerful is how real it is. She doesn't hide her scars; she shows them, and in doing so, gives other women permission to face their own truth. Every story, every prayer, every reflection in these pages feels like sitting across the table from her hearing her say, "You're not crazy. You're not alone. And you're going to make it."

I've watched my mom go from heartbreak to healing, from survival to purpose. And through it all, she's never lost her faith. Her journey reminds us that love isn't just something we find in someone else it's something we learn to nurture within ourselves.

So, as you turn these pages, I hope you feel what I feel: pride, peace, and the presence of a God who wastes nothing. Every detour, every tear, every prayer it's all part of becoming whole.

Mom, your story is more than a testimony. It's a ministry. And I know it's going to touch lives the same way your strength has touched mine.

With love,

Kailyn Serrano-Rivera Daughter & Witness to God's Restoration

Preface

I'm Kairy M. Springer—a woman who has walked through heartbreak, healing, and hard lessons, only to discover that every detour led me closer to God's purpose. Writing has always been my way of transforming pain into purpose, turning the pages of my life into testimonies of grace and growth.

I don't write from perfection—I write from process. My journey has been one of faith, forgiveness, and rediscovery. Through laughter, tears, and prayer, I've learned that peace is not negotiable, love should never cost your identity, and walking away is sometimes the most sacred act of self-respect.

My first book, *Caught in a Web of Lies*, was born from betrayal and became my first step toward freedom. *A Needle in a Haystack* continues that story—one that blends honesty, humor, and faith into a message of hope for every woman learning to love herself again.

I share my truth not because it's pretty, but because it's real. If my words can help another woman protect her peace, find her voice, or remember her worth, then every tear I shed was worth it.

My prayer is that my readers don't just see my story—they see their own healing through it. Because your peace is priceless. Your voice is sacred. And your story is far from over.

🙏 Opening Prayer

Heavenly Father,

Thank You for the gift of story—the way You turn broken pieces into testimonies of strength and hope. As these words are read, may they not only reflect my journey but also awaken courage in every heart that encounters them.

Lord, I ask that this book be more than pages and ink. Let it be a vessel of healing, a mirror of truth, and a reminder that no detour is wasted when it leads us closer to You. May each reader find themselves embraced by Your agape love, strengthened by Your promises, and empowered to reclaim their worth.

Father, I pray that laughter will lighten burdens, that honesty will break chains, and that prayer will open doors to peace. Let every testimony within these chapters point back to Your faithfulness—the One who transforms chaos into clarity and pain into purpose.

Bless every woman who turns these pages. Remind her that she is not defined by betrayal, disappointment, or loss, but by the unshakable love of Christ. May she walk boldly into the future You have prepared, knowing she is whole, worthy, and free.

In Jesus' name, **Amen.**

The Woman Revealed Within the Story

At one point or another, I believe every woman has fantasized, dreamed, or crafted her own vision of the perfect man. We imagine someone who embodies all our hopes, gentle yet strong, wise yet playful, romantic yet grounded. But the truth is, such perfection does not exist. No matter what we do or achieve, we will never attain flawlessness, nor will we ever find a flawless partner. We are all works in progress, shaped by time, trial, and grace.

Still, that hasn't stopped generations of women from dreaming. Across centuries, we've clung to the idea of "the one"—an idealized figure sculpted by our limited perspectives, societal expectations, media portrayals, and the environments that have surrounded us since birth. These influences have led us to believe that every story should end like the fairy tales we cherished as children.

What little girl hasn't imagined her wedding day? The colors—soft pinks and passionate reds. The sweet aroma of fresh flowers. Doves fluttering or butterflies dancing. The wind gently caressing her face, her hair flowing like a movie scene. The laughter of children in the background. And most of all, the piercing gaze of the one who will embrace her until the end of time. But as we grow older, reality begins to unravel the fantasy. Life is not picture perfect.

Take Cinderella, for example—one of my favorite fairy tales as a child. She's often portrayed as a victim of her stepmother and two cruel stepsisters. But now, I see her differently. Cinderella was a young girl who, through hardship and humility, was being shaped into a woman of substance. How else would she have learned responsibility if she hadn't been tasked with cooking and cleaning? How else would she have discovered that true beauty comes from within if she hadn't worn rags instead of gowns? How else would she have learned grace and hospitality if she hadn't catered to every whim of her household?

Those uncomfortable, even painful, experiences refined her. They prepared her to be a woman fit for a king.

Our lives aren't so different. Every situation God allows—whether a divine appointment or a detour of our own making, has a purpose. Each moment is part of the shaping. I remember the day my mother told my brother and me that she was giving us our inheritance. I was thrilled! Growing up, I always associated inheritance with money. But my mother had a different perspective.

She handed us each a piece of paper with our names written on it. Confused, we reached for them, and discovered they were chore lists. Each list detailed the tasks we were responsible for, the days they were to be done, and the standards by which they were to be completed.

That simple list was one of the first tools that began shaping who I am today. It taught me responsibility, trustworthiness, and work ethic. My mother may not have had wealth to pass down, but she understood the power of legacy. She was building a foundation, entrusting us with duties, expecting them to be done with excellence and timeliness.

In the same way, God has given us a divine inheritance: His Word. The Bible is our blueprint, our foundation, our guide. It contains clear instructions on how to live, love, and grow. Yet so often, we think we know better. We disregard His teachings, choosing our own paths and in doing so, we walk into experiences that shape us, sometimes painfully, but always purposefully.

"All Scripture is God-breathed and is useful for teaching, rebuking, correcting and training in righteousness." —2 Timothy 3:16

"The wise woman builds her house, but with her own hands the foolish one tears hers down." —Proverbs 14:1

"We are God's handiwork, created in Christ Jesus to do good works, which God prepared in advance for us to do." —Ephesians 2:10

So, as you read this journey—from fantasy to reality, from pain to purpose—I invite you to reflect on your own shaping. You are not broken. You are being built. And every trial, every chore, every detour is part of the divine design.

🙏 Reflective Prayer

Loving God,

Thank You for the gift of life's lessons—the ones wrapped in joy and the ones clothed in hardship. Just as Cinderella's trials shaped her into a woman fit for a king, I know that every circumstance You allow in my life is shaping me into the woman You have called me to be.

Forgive me for the times I have chased after perfection in others instead of seeking completeness in You. Remind me that no man, no dream, and no fairytale can ever replace the inheritance You have already given me—Your Word, Your wisdom, and Your unfailing love.

Lord, help me to embrace the responsibilities, detours, and challenges that come my way, knowing they are part of the foundation You are building in me. Teach me to trust Your process, to walk in obedience, and to see beauty in the refining.

May I never forget that true worth is not found in earthly fantasies, but in the eternal truth of Your promises. Guide me to live authentically, to love deeply, and to walk boldly in the purpose You have designed for me.

And as I continue this journey, let my story be a testimony that even in the midst of broken dreams, You are faithful to create something far greater than I could ever imagine.

In Jesus' name, **Amen.**

Agape Love

My journey has not been an easy ride. I've faced many emotional roller coasters, twists of heartbreak, loops of confusion, and valleys of disappointment. Yet through it all, I've tried to maintain a positive outlook, choosing to learn from each lesson along the way. I'll admit, some tests I've had to retake more than once. Growth isn't linear, and healing rarely comes without repetition. As I said before, we are all a work in progress. I am far from perfect, but I will continue to do my best until the day I rest in God's arms.

Each of us carries a story, marked by falls, failures, and fragile moments. But what a comfort it is to know that God's grace meets us anew every morning. His mercy never runs dry.

"My grace is sufficient for you, for my power is made perfect in weakness." —2 Corinthians 12:9 "Because of the Lord's great love we are not consumed, for his compassions never fail. They are new every morning." —Lamentations 3:22–23

Isn't it amazing? Despite our many faults, there is a God who loves us unconditionally. He is a forgiving Father. And though we may face the consequences of our choices, His discipline is always wrapped in love.

"For God so loved the world that He gave His one and only Son, that whoever believes in Him shall not perish but have eternal life." —John 3:16

In my first book, *Caught in a Web of Lies*, I shared the pain I endured—much of it self-inflicted. I chose to wear blinders and pursue an unhealthy relationship, ignoring the warning signs and silencing my inner voice. But even in that brokenness, I encountered the deepest love of God.

Growing up, I often heard about God's love. I never doubted it intellectually. But it wasn't until I found myself in the darkness that I truly experienced His embrace. I was hurting. I had disappointed Him. Yet His Holy Spirit wrapped around me like a warm blanket, whispering, "I'm here. I love you. I forgive you."

"The Lord our God is merciful and forgiving, even though we have rebelled against Him." —Daniel 9:9

I know I placed myself in that difficult situation. But if I hadn't walked through it, I wouldn't have understood the depth of agape love—love that is sacrificial, unconditional, and healing.

While I don't regret the experience itself, I do regret the choices I made within it. Still, I gained wisdom and maturity through the process. I learned about the vastness of God's love, but I also learned that His justice and holiness are not to be taken lightly. His love is not permissive, it is purifying.

This journey also reminded me of the power and necessity of forgiveness. No matter what others do to us, we are called to forgive. Not for their benefit, but for ours. Forgiveness frees our hearts from bitterness and keeps our connection with God flowing.

"For if you forgive other people when they sin against you, your heavenly Father will also forgive you. But if you do not forgive others their sins, your Father will not forgive your sins." —Matthew 6:14–15

Forgiveness doesn't mean allowing those who hurt us back into our lives. It means releasing them—letting go of the offense and entrusting justice to God. We forgive, we release, and we move forward. God will take care of the rest.

🙏 Reflective Prayer

Gracious Father,

Thank You for reminding me that Your love is greater than my failures, stronger than my pain, and deeper than any wound I have carried. Your Word says, *"My grace is sufficient for you, for My power is made perfect in weakness"* (*2 Corinthians 12:9*), and I have seen that truth unfold in my life.

Lord, I confess that I have stumbled many times, yet Your mercies are new every morning (*Lamentations 3:23*). Even when I disappointed You, Your Spirit wrapped me in comfort and whispered, *"I am here, I love you, and I forgive you"* (*Daniel 9:9*). Thank You for never abandoning me, even when I chose paths that led to pain.

Teach me to walk in the fullness of Your agape love—a love that forgives, heals, and restores. Help me to release resentment and bitterness, knowing that forgiveness is not weakness but freedom. As You have commanded, *"For if you forgive others their trespasses, your heavenly Father will also forgive you"* (*Matthew 6:14–15*).

Lord, let my life be a reflection of Your love. May I extend grace to others, not because they deserve it, but because You have freely given it to me. Let every trial I face become a testimony of Your faithfulness, and let every scar remind me of Your healing power.

I pray that I will continue to grow in wisdom and maturity, trusting Your justice and resting in Your embrace. May my journey always point back to You—the One who loved me first (*John 3:16*).

In Jesus' name, **Amen.**

Purification

Another woman who became fit for a king was Queen Esther. The Bible tells us that from the moment she was favored by the king, she entered a season of preparation. To stand before royalty, she had to be refined—inside and out. One of the first things the king provided was seven female attendants, along with special food and beauty treatments.

"Esther pleased him and won his favor. Immediately he provided her with beauty treatments and special food. He assigned to her seven female attendants selected from the king's palace and moved her and her attendants into the best place in the harem." —Esther 2:9

Esther's purification process lasted an entire year. For six months, she was treated with oil of myrrh—a symbol of healing and burial. The next six months were spent with perfumes and cosmetics, preparing her to meet the king.

"Before a young woman's turn came to go in to King Xerxes, she had to complete twelve months of beauty treatments prescribed for the women, six months with oil of myrrh and six with perfumes and cosmetics." —Esther 2:12

Just like Esther, we too need purification—but ours begins in the heart and mind. We often rush from one relationship to another, never pausing to examine how each experience has shaped us. We carry wounds, fears, and false beliefs into new chapters, unaware that healing requires intentional stillness.

One of the most powerful lessons I've learned on my journey is this: love yourself first. Take time to discover who you are. Learn to see yourself through God's eyes—not through the lens of past rejection or brokenness.

"I praise You because I am fearfully and wonderfully made; Your works are wonderful, I know that full well." —Psalm 139:14

Enjoy your own company. If you don't value time with yourself, how can you expect others to? Solitude is not loneliness—it's sacred space for restoration.

Breathe. When a relationship ends in pain, the last thing you want is to drag that emotional baggage into something new. Don't let your past bleed into your present. It's only fair to give the new person a clean slate. He shouldn't have to pay for the broken pieces left by someone else.

"Forget the former things; do not dwell on the past. See, I am doing a new thing!" —Isaiah 43:18–19

Healing is not just about moving on—it's about moving forward with clarity, grace, and wholeness. Like Esther, allow yourself to be purified. Let God prepare you—not just for a relationship, but for your divine purpose.

🙏 Reflective Prayer

Lord of Renewal,

Thank You for reminding me through Esther's story that preparation is sacred. Just as she underwent a season of purification before entering the king's presence, I too must allow You to purify my heart and mind before stepping into the future You have prepared for me.

Cleanse me from the residue of past hurts, broken relationships, and disappointments. Wash away bitterness, fear, and insecurity, and replace them with peace, confidence, and joy. Teach me to pause, reflect, and heal before moving forward, so that I do not carry yesterday's wounds into tomorrow's blessings.

Help me to see myself through Your eyes—worthy, loved, and whole. Remind me that solitude is not loneliness but an opportunity to grow closer to You and to discover the beauty of who I am in Christ.

Lord, breathe new life into me. Purify my thoughts, renew my spirit, and prepare me for the love, purpose, and destiny You have designed. May I walk boldly into new seasons, free from the baggage of the past, and ready to embrace the future with a heart that is healed and whole.

In Jesus' name, **Amen.**

Completeness

~✺~

I love chili—but the first time I tried to make it, I had no idea where to begin. I didn't know what ingredients were needed or how to layer the flavors. Thank God for Google! But even then, I found myself at a crossroads. There were so many recipes to choose from. Which one would be the tastiest? Which would come out thick and hearty? What if I used paprika—would it be too spicy?

In the same way, we often find ourselves at a crossroads when searching for Mr. Right. You may meet kind, respectful men, but that doesn't necessarily mean they're aligned with God's purpose for your life. Sometimes it feels like searching for a needle in a haystack. You know what you want—and what you won't compromise on—but still, many of us end up settling. It often takes multiple trials to arrive at the place we were meant to be from the start.

In my own search for that needle in the haystack, I've encountered a wide range of experiences, and so have many of my friends and family. Some brought joy, others brought tears. But just like the ingredients in chili, I believe each experience added flavor to our lives. Each one taught us something. These lessons have helped shape us into more complete individuals and continue to prepare us for the person God has chosen for us.

"Trust in the Lord with all your heart and lean not on your own understanding; in all your ways submit to Him, and He will make your paths straight." —Proverbs 3:5–6

My pastor once said, "Before you enter a relationship, you should be complete." That truth has stayed with me. Don't ever believe that someone else is going to complete you. This isn't *Jerry Maguire*! Completion is your responsibility. Happiness is not a gift someone else hands you, it's a choice you make daily, regardless of your circumstances.

"The joy of the Lord is your strength." —Nehemiah 8:10 "I have learned to be content whatever the circumstances." —Philippians 4:11

As we journey through life, we'll encounter situations that stretch us, challenge us, and help us grow. But it's up to us to pause, reflect, and ask: What needs to change in me? What do I need to learn to become whole?

Sadly, not everyone sees life this way. Some drown in disappointment, unable to extract the wisdom from their pain. But we must choose to focus. We must train our hearts to see each experience as a lesson. Ask yourself: What did I learn? Where has this taken me? Where is God leading me next?

"Consider it pure joy, my brothers and sisters, whenever you face trials of many kinds, because you know that the testing of your faith produces perseverance." —James 1:2–3

Life, like chili, is a blend of ingredients—some sweet, some spicy, some bitter. But when surrendered to God, even the most unexpected flavors can become part of a beautiful, nourishing whole.

🙏 Reflective Prayer

Blessed Redeemer,

Thank You for reminding me that true completeness does not come from another person, but from You alone. Just as every ingredient adds flavor to a recipe, every experience— whether joyful or painful—adds depth to my life and prepares me for the future You have designed.

Lord, help me to embrace the lessons hidden in each trial and to see them not as setbacks but as seasoning for my soul. Teach me to stand firm in my values, to resist the temptation to settle, and to trust that Your timing is perfect.

I confess that at times I have looked to others to fill the empty spaces within me, but today I choose to find my wholeness in You. Remind me daily that happiness is my decision, not someone else's responsibility.

Guide me at every crossroad, Lord. When choices feel overwhelming, grant me discernment to choose the path that aligns with Your purpose. Let my completeness be rooted in Your love, so that when the right person comes into my life, I meet them not in brokenness but in strength.

May my journey reflect Your faithfulness, and may my heart remain steadfast in the truth that I am already whole in You.

In Jesus' name, **Amen.**

Mr. Wrong: When Familiar Mistakes Wear New Faces

~⸎~

At some point in life, most of us have encountered a variety of men—some charming, some confusing, and some downright disastrous. Have you ever met Mr. Wrong? Mr. Psycho? Mr. Cheap? Mr. Lazy? Mr. Addiction? Mr. Gambler? Mr. Detour? The list goes on…

Let me be clear: I'm not here to generalize or say that all men are the same. This is simply a reflection of my own journey, along with the stories shared by friends and family. So buckle up—the ride might get bumpy. Or maybe it'll make you laugh, cry, reminisce… and if the shoe fits, well, you know what to do.

Who hasn't met Mr. Wrong? According to the Free Dictionary, Mr. Right is defined as "the man who would make an ideal mate." So, it's safe to say Mr. Wrong is… not that. But it's deeper than definitions. In the song "Mr. Wrong" by Drake and Mary J. Blige, she sings about how good it feels to be with Mr. Wrong—even though it breaks her heart. Can we call him a heartbreaker?

She also refers to him as a "bad boy." Why are we so drawn to bad boys? Sometimes it feels like we have a magnet for dysfunction. Or maybe we're the ones chasing it.

So, what makes Mr. Wrong so wrong? Is it his actions? His lifestyle? His emotional availability? Or is it simply that he's not aligned with God's purpose for us?

Truthfully, Mr. Wrong is different for every woman. He might be unemployed, emotionally unavailable, too clingy, too distant, too short, too tall, too passive, too aggressive— the list is endless. I bet we could fill an entire dictionary with each woman's definition of Mr. Wrong.

Have you ever felt like you keep receiving the same package in a different gift wrap? You're not alone. Many of us find ourselves in a vicious cycle—repeating patterns, attracting the same kind of man, and wondering why. Is Mr. Wrong really the problem? Or are we the ones choosing him over and over again?

Breaking the cycle starts with self-examination. I had to ask myself: What am I doing that keeps leading me back to places I don't want to be? What needs to change in me?

One book that deeply impacted me was *The Power of a Praying Wife* by Stormie Omartian. She writes that one of the first steps in transformation is acknowledging that change begins with us. She prayed daily for God to change her heart and to help her see her spouse through His eyes. That perspective is powerful. If we could see others through God's eyes, we'd approach relationships with more grace, wisdom, and discernment.

"Do not conform to the pattern of this world, but be transformed by the renewing of your mind." —Romans 12:2 "Above all else, guard your heart, for everything you do flows from it." —Proverbs 4:23

I've read countless articles, devotionals, and books—including the Bible. I've listened to testimonies, sermons, and the wisdom of my pastor. But most importantly, I've learned to seek God's face daily. Yes—daily. One of my constant prayers has been, "Thy will be done." Hillary Scott's song by that title became my lifeline. Whenever I felt overwhelmed or tempted to take control, I played that song.

I needed to be reminded that God's will is better than mine—even when my emotions screamed otherwise.

"Not my will, but Yours be done." —Luke 22:42 "Be still, and know that I am God." —Psalm 46:10

Let's be honest—God doesn't need our help. I've learned that the hard way. I've taken matters into my own hands, only to end up pleading with God to rescue me from the mess I created. But when we cultivate a daily relationship with Him, everything changes. The Holy Spirit begins to guide us. Our spiritual eyes and ears open. We start to see things differently.

"But when He, the Spirit of truth, comes, He will guide you into all the truth." —John 16:13

I don't know about you, but I'm tired—and honestly, afraid—of making the same mistake again. Each morning, we have a choice: follow the map we've drawn for ourselves, or turn on the GPS—God's Perfect System. One leads to our own path. The other leads to His purpose.

Which one do you want?

The truth about Mr. Wrong is that sometimes we stay in relationships we know aren't right. Why? Fear. Time invested. Disappointment. Low self-esteem. Convenience. Finances. Loneliness. Routine. The reasons are many. But the question remains: Is Mr. Wrong really wrong? Or did we settle for something we knew wasn't right from the beginning?

Are we taking matters into our own hands?

"There is a way that appears to be right, but in the end it leads to death." —Proverbs 14:12 "The steps of a good man are ordered by the Lord, and He delights in his way." —Psalm 37:23

Let's stop settling. Let's start surrendering. Let's break the cycle—not by chasing perfection, but by pursuing purpose.

What did I learn?

I learned that healing starts with honesty. That change begins with me. That God's guidance is better than any plan I could ever create. And that Mr. Wrong isn't just a person—it's a pattern. One I'm finally ready to break.

🙏 Reflective Prayer

Eternal Father,

Thank You for opening my eyes to the patterns that have kept me bound to "Mr. Wrong." Too often I have repeated the same mistakes, chasing after what looked good on the outside but left me broken within. Yet through every disappointment, You have been faithful to remind me that healing begins with honesty and that true change begins with You.

Lord, I surrender my choices, my desires, and my relationships to Your will. Teach me to see others through Your eyes, not through the lens of my loneliness or fear. Help me to break free from cycles of settling and to walk boldly in the path You have prepared for me.

I confess that I have tried to take control, but I now choose to trust Your GPS—Your Perfect System—to guide me. Open my spiritual eyes and ears so that I may discern Your voice above all others. Let my heart be aligned with Your purpose, and let my steps be ordered by Your Spirit.

Father, I ask for the courage to let go of what is not meant for me and the wisdom to embrace the lessons each experience has taught. May I never again confuse temporary attraction with lasting love. Instead, let me rest in the assurance that Your plan is greater than any I could create.

Thank You for reminding me that Mr. Wrong is not just a person but a pattern—and with You, I have the power to break it.

In Jesus' name, **Amen.**

Mr. Psycho: When Charm Turns into Chaos

He might look perfect—head to toe, inside and out—until he opens his mouth or finds himself in a situation where the real beast emerges. Charm can be deceiving. And while most dictionaries define a "psycho" as someone mentally unstable or irrational, personal experience paints a much broader picture.

One of my daughters defines a psycho as someone who constantly interrogates you—asking strange questions, tracking your every move, and imagining things that aren't there. My other daughter calls him a stalker—someone who does "crazy stuff" that makes your skin crawl. Just like Mr. Wrong, every woman has her own definition of what a psycho looks like. But one adjective seems universal: crazy.

To me, a psycho is a dangerous blend of behaviors—ranging from pathological lying to violent tendencies. I remember a story a friend told me: she was driving a date home, someone she'd just met and was still getting to know. Out of nowhere, he blurted, "I can see dead people." And no, he wasn't quoting the lines of Haley Joel Osment in the movie *The Sixth Sense*. Crazy! I give her credit for finishing that drive. If it were me, I'd have pulled over and said, "The dead people say get out of my car."

Needless to say, she never saw him again.

But have you ever encountered a *passive* psycho? I define this type as calculated, quiet, and deceptive. They hide things well—sometimes for months. But eventually, they slip. And when they do, it's like a bomb going off. You find yourself six months into a relationship, only to discover his criminal record is longer than the Missouri River.

I met one of those once. He presented himself as a Christian, a gentleman, a professional, a published author, a former athlete, and a devoted father. I thought I'd hit the jackpot. But his biggest mistake was introducing me to his family. That's when the mask began to crack. Nothing added up. Long story short—he had fabricated an entire life to hide the truth: multiple criminal charges and a traumatic past that had left deep emotional scars.

When he was finally exposed, the beast came out. Death threats. Manipulation. Intimidation. He tried everything to hurt me. But thank God—*literally*—for His protection.

"The Lord is faithful, and He will strengthen you and protect you from the evil one." —2 Thessalonians 3:3 "No weapon formed against you shall prosper." —Isaiah 54:17

Can you spot a psycho? Maybe. Maybe not. Sometimes the signs are obvious—like "I see dead people." Other times, you're months into a relationship, sensing something's off but unable to pinpoint it. That's why it's *critical* to stay in God's presence. I always ask for discernment. And even when I ignored the signs, God was faithful to reveal the truth.

"If any of you lacks wisdom, you should ask God, who gives generously to all without finding fault." —James 1:5 "The Spirit of truth will guide you into all truth." —John 16:13

Discernment is not just a spiritual gift—it's a survival tool. When emotions cloud our judgment, God's voice becomes our compass. He sees what we cannot. He knows what's hidden. And He will always be faithful to expose what's meant to protect us.

What did I learn?

I learned not to believe everything I hear. I learned to take my time, explore situations, and guard my heart. I learned to ask God for direction—even when it seems petty. How does he act around your friends? What about his own friends? How does he speak about his parents—especially his mother and his relationship with women? Is he truly a devoted father, or is child support chasing him? Does he have a daily relationship with God, or does he only pray at restaurants to impress?

Watch for the little signs. They're always there. And when you see them—don't ignore them.

🙏 Reflective Prayer

Faithful Protector,

Thank You for shielding me when danger tried to disguise itself as love. Thank You for opening my eyes to the truth, even when I ignored the signs You placed before me. Lord, I acknowledge that charm without character is deception, and I ask You to continue to guard my heart from those who seek to manipulate, control, or harm.

Grant me discernment, Father. Teach me to recognize the subtle signs that reveal a person's true nature. Help me to pause, to listen to Your Spirit, and to trust Your warnings even when my emotions try to silence them.

I confess that I have believed words that were empty and promises that were false, but I now choose to lean on Your truth. Your Word says, *"But the Lord is faithful, and He will strengthen you and protect you from the evil one"* (*2 Thessalonians 3:3*). I rest in that promise, knowing You are my shield and my refuge.

Lord, purify my relationships. Surround me with people who reflect Your love, integrity, and peace. Remove those who wear masks of charm but carry chaos in their hearts. Let me never again settle for appearances, but instead seek the fruit of the Spirit in those I allow close to me.

Thank You for turning what was meant to harm me into wisdom that now protects me. May my testimony remind others that You are faithful, that discernment is a gift, and that no mask can hide the truth from You.

In Jesus' name, **Amen.**

Mr. Cheap: When Frugality Turns into Freeloading

When the word *cheap* comes to mind, I picture someone who refuses to spend their own money but has no problem letting others foot the bill. I also think of someone who's so restrictive that they deny themselves even the smallest pleasures—like a piece of their favorite chocolate. According to Merriam-Webster, a cheap person is "stingy"—like Ebenezer Scrooge himself.

Growing up, I used to hear the joke: *"He won't buy a soda because he doesn't want to waste the gas by burping."* Ha! That paints the picture, doesn't it?

A friend of mine once dated a man for two months. And let me tell you, it didn't take long before she started wondering: *Is he frugal… or just looking for a sugar mama?* Within two weeks, he asked her for gas money. Two weeks! She barely knew him. Then came the Dollar Store incident. As they approached the checkout line, he looked at her like she was supposed to pay for his items. One dollar, y'all. One dollar.

Another time, he invited her to his friend's birthday party—then asked her to buy the birthday card. *Excuse me?* It was *his* friend. She didn't even know the guy! A month into the relationship, he popped the question—over text. No ring. No plan. Just a proposal. Naturally, she said no.

But he didn't stop there. Next, he asked to move in. Now, she's a kind woman, but she doesn't run a hotel or a boarding house. Then came the movie date—except she ended up paying for her own ticket *and* her popcorn.

Now, don't get me wrong. I believe in equality. I've paid for dinners. I've treated people I've dated. I don't believe in taking advantage of anyone. But if *you* invite me out, I believe it's your responsibility to cover it. That's just basic courtesy.

And it didn't stop. One day, he came over to visit and brought his laundry. Was he there to see her—or did he think her house was a laundromat? And for her birthday? Not even a 50-cent card. Nothing. If you can't afford a card, be creative! Grab a napkin or a piece of toilet paper and write something heartfelt. It's not about the money, it's about the effort.

Honestly, I think she held on to that relationship far too long. The marriage proposal after one month should've been a flashing red light with sirens: *Run, girl, run!*

"Do not give dogs what is sacred; do not throw your pearls to pigs. If you do, they may trample them under their feet, and turn and tear you to pieces." —Matthew 7:6 "Above all else, guard your heart, for everything you do flows from it." —Proverbs 4:23

There's a difference between being frugal and being selfish. Frugality is wise stewardship. Cheapness, especially when it leans on others while offering nothing in return, is a red flag. Relationships should be built on mutual respect, generosity, and shared responsibility, not manipulation or freeloading.

"Each of you should give what you have decided in your heart to give, not reluctantly or under compulsion, for God loves a cheerful giver." —2 Corinthians 9:7

So, where do we draw the line? Right at the point where your dignity, peace, and self-worth are compromised. Don't ignore the signs. Don't excuse the patterns. And don't settle for someone who treats you like a convenience instead of a blessing.

What did she learn?

She learned that you don't truly know someone until you spend time with them. She realized the importance of setting boundaries early and recognizing red flags before they become patterns. Most importantly, she learned that generosity in a relationship should be mutual—not one-sided. And yes, she joked that she needed to invest in a good pair of running shoes for next time.

These experiences helped her define what she could and couldn't live with in a relationship. While some people might be okay with being a "sugar mama," she knew that wasn't the life she wanted. Mr. Cheap taught her that love should never come with a price and that self-respect is worth far more than any dollar item.

🙏 Reflective Prayer

Provider God,

Thank You for reminding me that true love is not measured in dollars, gifts, or material things, but in sacrifice, generosity, and mutual care. Lord, I confess that at times I have overlooked red flags, hoping that love would outweigh selfishness. But You have shown me that relationships built on imbalance and taking advantage of others are not rooted in Your design.

Father, teach me to set healthy boundaries and to recognize when someone's actions do not align with their words. Help me to value myself enough to walk away from relationships that drain me instead of nurture me. Remind me that I am worthy of love that gives, not just takes.

Lord, I ask for discernment to see the difference between frugality and selfishness, between wisdom and exploitation. Let me never confuse stinginess with stewardship. Surround me with people who understand that generosity is not about money alone, but about time, effort, and heart.

Thank You for the lessons that even painful experiences bring. Thank You for showing me that self-respect is priceless and that love should never come with a cost tag. May I carry these truths forward, walking in confidence, knowing that You will provide relationships that reflect Your goodness and balance.

In Jesus' name, **Amen.**

Mr. Lazy: When Excuses Outweigh Effort

Oh, Mr. Lazy. According to Webster's Dictionary, he's someone who is underactive, sluggish, and unwilling to work or use energy. But my personal favorite definition? "Work-shy." Ha! That one hits the nail on the head.

Let's be real—we've all had lazy days. I call them "mental days" or "vegetative states," and I enjoy them guilt-free. But there's a difference between taking a break and being allergic to work. Unfortunately, I've met a few men who fall into the latter category. One in particular? He topped the cake.

When I first met Mr. Lazy, he told me he was a salesperson. Seemed legit—until three weeks later, he confessed he'd been fired because his job conflicted with his "entertainment hobby." Red flag! I started to wonder if he even had a job when we met. Still, I tried to be supportive. I encouraged him to apply elsewhere, even helped him search for opportunities. I didn't want to seem shallow by walking away just because he was unemployed. But as time passed, nothing changed.

Eventually, after weeks of nudging, he told me he had an interview at a local hotel. On the day of the interview, he called to say he got the job. I was thrilled! But then came the "but." Training wouldn't start until the first week of June. Mind you, this was the end of April. Odd, right? Still, I gave him the benefit of the doubt. He picked up a few odd jobs here and there, and yes—I know what you're thinking: *She's still with him?* Let me remind you, I've made my share of mistakes. This was one of them. And in my defense, it was an on-and-off relationship.

The day before his supposed training, I asked if he was ready. His response? "I'm not sure I want to go." I was livid. I told him plainly, "If you want a future with me, you need to find a job." I hoped that would light a fire under him. It didn't. His excuse? The job would interfere with his entertainment career. I was so upset I didn't speak to him for days.

He kept calling, texting, saying he "loved" me and promising to change. He said I was right and that he'd find another job. That week, I was heading out of town to visit family. Before I left, I sent him info about a job fair. He claimed he went, got an interview, and even sent me a picture of himself dressed up in the car. Later, he texted: "I got hired!" This was the first week of June. But—surprise—training wouldn't start until the end of the month. Again.

At this point, I should've been done. But I waited. On the day he was supposed to start, he texted saying he needed to talk. When I called, he said, "They changed the training schedule. It's now in two weeks. But I think I'm just going to find another job." I was beyond frustrated.

Now, did I mention I have detective instincts? I Googled the company. First red flag: the street he gave me didn't exist. I called the company anyway. They told me there was no training scheduled and no record of him. When I confronted him, he didn't apologize. Instead, he gave me the company's number and told me to apply for a job myself to verify the info. Really? I already had a job. I didn't need to apply anywhere.

That was the moment I finally saw him for who he was: a man with no drive, no goals, and no intention of changing. He never admitted the truth. To this day, I'm sure he'd still deny lying. But I opened my eyes, stopped trusting him, and walked away. He wasn't looking for a partner—he was looking for a provider.

"The soul of the sluggard craves and gets nothing, while the soul of the diligent is richly supplied." —Proverbs 13:4 "If anyone is not willing to work, let him not eat." —2 Thessalonians 3:10

Relationships require effort, vision, and shared responsibility. Love is not a license for laziness. If someone consistently chooses excuses over action, they're not building a future—they're draining yours.

"Do two walk together unless they have agreed to do so?" —Amos 3:3

Sometimes, the hardest part isn't spotting the red flags—it's admitting we ignored them. But grace gives us the strength to learn, grow, and move on. And when we do, we make room for someone who's not just willing to walk beside us— but to build with us.

What Did I Learn?

I learned that being supportive doesn't mean sacrificing your peace. I realized that holding on to someone who has no place in your future only brings unnecessary chaos. Vulnerability can blind us to reality, making us create comforting illusions instead of facing the truth. That's why maintaining a daily relationship with God is essential—His guidance helps us see clearly when emotions cloud our judgment.

I often tell my daughters that every decision, good or bad, carries consequences. Through this experience, I learned to think through each step carefully and to stop investing in someone who wasn't investing in himself. Support from a distance is still support—but it doesn't require self-sacrifice.

🙏 Reflective Prayer

Gracious Lord,

Thank You for teaching me that love is not meant to be carried on one set of shoulders. True partnership requires effort, responsibility, and commitment. Lord, I confess that in my desire to be supportive, I sometimes ignored the truth and held on longer than I should have. Yet You were faithful to open my eyes and remind me that peace is more valuable than empty promises.

Father, help me to discern the difference between genuine struggle and willful laziness. Teach me to encourage others without sacrificing my own well-being. Remind me that support does not mean enabling, and compassion does not mean carrying someone else's unwillingness to grow.

Lord, I ask for wisdom to guide my children and those around me, showing them that every decision carries consequences. May they learn to invest in people who invest in themselves, and to walk away from those who drain their spirit.

Thank You for reminding me that vulnerability must be balanced with discernment, and that illusions cannot replace truth. Keep me rooted in Your Word, so that when emotions cloud my judgment, Your Spirit brings clarity.

I choose today to protect my peace, to honor my worth, and to trust that You will align me with relationships that reflect effort, growth, and love.

In Jesus' name, **Amen.**

Mr. Addiction: When the Bottle Speaks Louder Than Love

A friend of mine once found herself in a relationship that tested her boundaries, her values, and her emotional resilience. Her boyfriend, though charming and affectionate at times, had a complicated relationship with alcohol. Early on, he confessed to having received a DUI—claiming it was due to refusing a breath test and having alcohol found in his car. He assured her that drinking wasn't a problem, and she chose to believe him.

But actions speak louder than words.

During a night out with friends, his behavior told a very different story. He drank excessively, became incoherent, spent money recklessly, and couldn't even sign his name properly. The scene was disturbing. It triggered memories of a past relationship that had left her emotionally scarred. She tried to talk to him, hoping for accountability. Instead, he deflected with, "I'm not perfect."

"As a dog returns to its vomit, so fools repeat their folly." — Proverbs 26:11

The next day, she approached him calmly. She wasn't judging—she was setting a boundary. She explained that she couldn't allow alcohol to be a part of her life. She gave him a choice: her or the drinking. He chose her, promising to stop because he understood it wasn't healthy.

But promises without transformation are just words.

Just a week later, he visited her with his daughter. While she was cleaning, he took the child to a nearby playground. When they returned, she noticed his daughter inside watching TV—but he was nowhere to be found. She stepped outside and found him drinking again. Once more, he offered excuses and tried to shift the blame, even pointing out her imperfections.

She was furious. She told him that once he sobered up, he needed to leave. His ego flared, and he wanted to leave immediately. But she insisted he wait until he was sober— especially with his daughter present. He eventually calmed down and stayed the night. But the next morning, he denied everything. He refused to admit he had a problem.

That was the breaking point.

She ended the relationship. It was clear that alcohol was his first love—and she couldn't compete with that. She felt deep sorrow for his daughter, knowing her journey with him might be a difficult one.

"Do not be misled: 'Bad company corrupts good character.'" —1 Corinthians 15:33 "Have nothing to do with the fruitless deeds of darkness, but rather expose them." —Ephesians 5:11

Walking away wasn't easy. But it was necessary. She chose peace over chaos, truth over denial, and healing over heartbreak. She realized that love should never require you to compromise your values or compete with addiction.

"The Lord is close to the brokenhearted and saves those who are crushed in spirit." —Psalm 34:18

What did she learn?

She learned that love cannot thrive where addiction reigns. She realized that promises made under pressure often lack sincerity. Most importantly, she learned to trust her instincts and uphold her boundaries. Her experience reminded her that no one is perfect, but imperfection should never be used as an excuse to continue harmful behavior. She walked away more strongly, knowing that protecting her peace was more important than preserving a broken relationship.

🙏 Reflective Prayer

Merciful Father,

Thank You for teaching me that love cannot survive where addiction takes control. Thank You for giving me the strength to recognize when promises are empty and when boundaries must be upheld. Lord, I confess that at times I wanted to believe words instead of actions, but You reminded me that true love is proven through responsibility, sacrifice, and respect.

Father, I pray for those bound by addiction. Break the chains that hold them captive and heal the wounds that drive them to destructive choices. Bring restoration where there is brokenness, and peace where there is chaos.

Lord, help me to trust my instincts when Your Spirit warns me. Teach me to protect my peace and to walk away from relationships that dishonor You. Remind me that imperfection is part of being human, but it should never be used as an excuse to continue harmful behavior.

Thank You for showing me that boundaries are not walls of fear but shields of wisdom. Thank You for reminding me that my worth is not measured by someone else's choices, but by Your love for me.

I choose today to walk in strength, to honor the lessons You've given me, and to trust that You will align me with relationships that reflect Your truth.

In Jesus' name, **Amen.**

Mr. Gambler: When the Dice Roll Over Love

A close friend of mine endured a heartbreaking relationship with a man whose addiction to gambling consumed every part of their life together. At first, the signs were subtle—he would disappear for days, always returning with apologies and promises to change. But addiction doesn't shrink; it grows. And his did.

It escalated to the point where he began pawning household items—ceiling fans, closet doors, anything he could get his hands on—just to feed his habit. She tried everything to help him see the damage he was causing. She pleaded, reasoned, prayed. But he refused to admit he had a problem, let alone seek help. Eventually, she had no choice but to file for divorce.

The breaking point came in a moment of vulnerability and pain.

One night, she was bitten by a spider and had to be rushed to the emergency room. He drove her there, but when she was called in, he chose to stay in the lobby. Inside, the doctor had to cut open her thigh, insert a drainage tube, and leave the wound open to allow the poison to escape. She was in excruciating pain, heavily medicated with codeine, and barely able to walk.

When she was finally discharged, weak and disoriented, she stepped into the lobby—only to find he had deserted her.

She called him several times. No answer. Embarrassed and ashamed, she didn't call anyone else. Instead, she began walking to the nearest gas station—five blocks away, in the dark, wearing short shorts, limping in pain, and disoriented from the medication. Men slowed down as they passed, mistaking her for someone selling herself. She finally reached the gas station and collapsed on the sidewalk, crying and praying for help.

And God answered.

A kind woman saw her and offered to take her home. That moment of grace reminded her that even in abandonment, God never leaves us.

"Even though I walk through the darkest valley, I will fear no evil, for You are with me." —Psalm 23:4 "The Lord is near to the brokenhearted and saves the crushed in spirit." —Psalm 34:18

Her husband didn't return for three days. When he did, he showed no remorse. Even after seven years of divorce, he still struggles with gambling—now worsened by alcohol and drugs. After three years of separation and multiple chances, he had the audacity to say she hadn't waited long enough.

"As a dog returns to its vomit, so fools repeat their folly." —Proverbs 26:11 "Do not be yoked together with unbelievers. For what do righteousness and wickedness have in common?" —2 Corinthians 6:14

Her story is a sobering reminder that addiction is not just a personal struggle—it's a relational one. It affects everyone connected to it. And sometimes, love means letting go. Not out of bitterness, but out of survival.

She chose healing. She chose peace. She chose to stop competing with a destructive addiction that had become his first love.

"You will keep in perfect peace those whose minds are steadfast, because they trust in You." —Isaiah 26:3

What did she learn?

She learned that addiction, when left unchecked, can destroy not only the addict but everyone around them. She learned that love cannot survive without trust, safety, and mutual respect. Most importantly, she learned that peace is not found in a partner—it is found in God. Today, she remains single, not because she's bitter, but because she values peace over chaos. And in her words, "God's peace surpasses any understanding."

🙏 Reflective Prayer

Prince of Peace,

Thank You for reminding me that true love cannot exist without trust, safety, and respect. Lord, I have seen how addiction can consume not only the one bound by it but also the hearts of those who love them. Yet even in the darkest moments, You have proven Yourself faithful, sending help when it was most needed and covering me with Your peace.

Father, I release the pain of abandonment, betrayal, and disappointment into Your hands. Heal the wounds left behind by broken promises and selfish choices. Teach me to value peace over chaos, and to never again confuse endurance with acceptance of harm.

Lord, I ask for strength to walk away from what destroys me and courage to stand firm in the boundaries You have called me to set. Remind me that my worth is not defined by someone else's struggles, but by Your love that never fails.

Thank You for showing me that peace is not found in another person but in You alone. Your Word declares, *"And the peace of God, which surpasses all understanding, will guard your hearts and your minds in Christ Jesus"* (*Philippians 4:7*). I choose to rest in that promise today.

May my story be a testimony that even when love falters, Your peace remains unshakable.

In Jesus' name, **Amen.**

Kairy M. Springer

Mr. Cheater: When the Bet Was My Heart

I was thirsty. Yes—*thirsty*. What I really wanted was a strawberry cheesecake milkshake, rich and satisfying. But in my desperation, I settled for water. And that moment became a metaphor for my journey.

I had reached a point in life where I deeply longed for that special someone. I wanted companionship, connection, and love. But in my longing, I neglected to measure the consequences of settling. I reconnected with an old flame and thought, *This is it.* I believed I had finally arrived at my happy ending. The obstacles that once stood between us were gone. We could finally be together.

But instead of a fairytale, I ended up with a broken heart. Why did I think this time would be different?

One day, while shopping at Walmart with my daughter, I bumped into him. Butterflies filled my stomach. All I wanted was to kiss him and hold him tight—but I held back. We talked briefly and went our separate ways. Then, in the parking lot, we bumped into each other again.

He was now a business owner and offered his services. My defense mechanism is sarcasm, so when he pitched his business again, all I wanted to say was, *I have road assistance.* But I gave him my number, and he gave me his.

That afternoon, he messaged me. He asked if I was in a relationship and invited me to dinner. And just like that, the flame was rekindled. We talked constantly, went out often, and even took a two-day beach vacation. Everything seemed perfect—or so I thought.

By the second month, things began to shift. Our outings became fewer. Texts turned into a one-way street. I started to feel taken for granted.

When I expressed my feelings, he said business was struggling and he needed time to fix things. I tried to be patient and supportive. But after four months, things only got worse. He barely called, rarely showed up, and began ignoring me altogether.

Red flags started waving. He frequently received calls from another woman but never answered when I was around. When I asked, he claimed she was just a client. But the calls continued—month after month.

Once his business picked up again, so did his services. One day, while I was in his car, she called again. He ignored it. I stayed silent, but my "detective mode" switched on.

I discovered she was the woman he had dated before me. My mind raced. If their relationship had truly ended six months before we started dating, why was she still calling so persistently? The only explanation: they were still seeing each other. He had been lying to me for months.

I began connecting the dots. I remembered seeing a text from a woman sticking her tongue out. When I asked, he brushed it off—said she was just a family friend who liked to joke. I stayed quiet, but the distrust lingered.

Then came the roses and the teddy bear. A huge white bear with a red bow and a bouquet of red roses. He claimed it was a client's gift of appreciation. I might've believed that if it had been a gift card—but roses and a teddy bear? That was personal.

I confronted him. I gave him the chance to end things respectfully. I told him, *If you want to be with someone else, opt me out. I refuse to be disrespected.* He lied to my face. He knew he was cheating, yet he held on. Later, I realized he was just using me.

"The heart is deceitful above all things and beyond cure. Who can understand it?" —Jeremiah 17:9 "Do not be deceived: God cannot be mocked. A man reaps what he sows." —Galatians 6:7

I couldn't understand. We had talked about marriage, about building a future. How could he hurt me again?

I was in so much pain. I stopped eating. Stopped calling. Stopped texting. He didn't even notice—he was too busy spending time with her.

Sometimes he'd call once a day, acting like everything was fine. When he asked about my plans, I wondered: *Did he care—or was he just making sure we wouldn't bump into each other while he was with her?*

One day, at his place, he said he had errands and would return later. I waited for hours. But my instincts kicked in again. I already knew where she lived, so I drove there.

And there he was.

Hallelujah for Google! Did you know Google is a snitch? Ha ha…

"You will know the truth, and the truth will set you free." — John 8:32 "Above all else, guard your heart, for everything you do flows from it." —Proverbs 4:23

Settling for less than God's best will always leave you thirsty. I wanted the milkshake. I settled for water. But now, I know better. I won't ignore the signs. I won't silence my intuition. And I won't trade my worth for temporary affection.

What did I learn?

I learned that the past should stay in the past—if it didn't work then, it won't work now. I learned to trust my instincts, because when something doesn't feel right, it's usually because it isn't. I learned that even though I loved him deeply, I love myself more, and while he thought he had both of us, he ended up losing everything and standing empty-handed. I realized that being a provider is not the same as being a partner, and gifts cannot replace honesty or respect. I came to understand that heartbreak is also preparation— that we must experience the wrong one to truly value the right one. As Mandy Hale wrote, *"He was never meant to be my great love. Or even a love at all. He was just meant to get me ready for it."* Most of all, I learned that healing takes time, but I rose again, because falling is part of living and staying down is only temporary.

🙏 Reflective Prayer

Faithful Father,

Thank You for reminding me that heartbreak is not the end of my story, but part of the preparation for the love and purpose You have designed for me. Lord, I confess that I once believed the past could be rewritten, but You have shown me that what is broken cannot always be repaired— and that sometimes letting go is the greatest act of love for myself.

Father, heal the wounds left by betrayal and dishonesty. Restore my trust, not in man, but in You—the One who never lies, never abandons, and never fails. Teach me to value honesty and respect above empty gifts or promises. Remind me that being a provider is not the same as being a partner, and that true love reflects Your sacrificial, faithful nature.

Lord, I thank You for the strength to rise again after falling. Your Word declares, *"The Lord is close to the brokenhearted and saves those who are crushed in spirit"* (*Psalm 34:18*). I hold onto that promise, knowing that You are near in my pain and present in my healing.

Help me to trust my instincts when Your Spirit warns me, and to walk away from what dishonors my worth. May I never again settle for less than the love You intend for me. Let my scars become testimonies of resilience, and let my story inspire others to choose themselves, to choose peace, and to choose You.

Thank You for turning heartbreak into wisdom, and for preparing me to recognize and cherish the right one when he comes.

In Jesus' name, **Amen.**

Mr. Detour: When Choosing Myself Was the Only Way Forward

Didn't I tell you? Life has a way of testing you—again and again—until you finally see the truth and pass the test. And just like Britney Spears said, *"Oops!... I did it again."* I thought I had met *the one.* Wait—haven't I said that before? Ha! Yes, I truly believed it this time.

After swearing off dating apps and convincing myself I was done, I found myself scrolling through Facebook Dating. One profile caught my eye. He seemed like my "type": tall, dark, and—at least to my then-blind perspective—handsome. I messaged him, determined to ask all the right questions this time.

We dove into back-to-back conversations. He told me he had four children, had lived in St. Croix, and had been married twice. But after our divorce, I learned the truth: he had five children, and I was actually his *fourth* wife. At the time, I took his words at face value. The truth didn't surface until much later.

"The Lord detests lying lips, but He delights in people who are trustworthy." —Proverbs 12:22

Our first date was dinner at Bahama Breeze. It was lovely. We followed it with more dates—Disney Springs, the beach, Miami, local vacations, motorcycle rides, badminton, and many other outings. It felt like a dream. Or maybe, like the saying goes, *"too good to be true."*

Then came the first crack.

Around July, before he moved in, a woman messaged me on Facebook. She claimed she had been with him just a week before we started dating and even sent me explicit photos he had sent her. I confronted him. He swore it was before we met. I wanted to believe him—her stories weren't consistent—so I did.

As the months passed, I fell deeper.

I asked early on if he was married. He said no. But by October, after we had decided he would move in, he admitted he was still married—though he claimed he had been separated for five years. Another lie.

He spoke often of his two minor children, saying they lived mostly with him because their mother—whom he insisted he had never married—was dying of cancer. He described her fainting, bedridden, unable to care for them. I felt compassion for her. Later, I would learn the truth.

"For nothing is hidden that will not be made manifest, nor is anything secret that will not be known and come to light." —Luke 8:17

I should have walked away. But I didn't.

I stayed. Not because I didn't see the truth, but because I wasn't ready to accept it. I clung to hope—that love could rewrite reality, that loyalty could heal what deception had broken. I told myself grace meant staying. That compassion meant enduring. But deep down, I was unraveling—spiritually, emotionally, silently.

"Hope deferred makes the heart sick, but a longing fulfilled is a tree of life." —Proverbs 13:12 "Above all else, guard your heart, for everything you do flows from it." —Proverbs 4:23

Exactly one year after we met—and after his divorce—we got married.

It felt like a fairytale. We married twice: once at the courthouse on the anniversary of our first conversation, and again on the anniversary of our first date. The second wedding was beautiful—a lakeside ceremony with sand, white and red decorations, family, friends, and his children. I wore a Cinderella-style gown with red roses and a tiara. My grandkids wore white shirts with red roses. As I walked down the aisle, *"Thinking Out Loud"* by Ed Sheeran played.

It was magical.

"There is a time for everything, and a season for every activity under the heavens." —Ecclesiastes 3:1 "The heart of man plans his way, but the Lord establishes his steps." —Proverbs 16:9

But the magic didn't last.

Once we were married, the mask fell off. He had portrayed himself as kind, loving, always serving, and attentive in front of others—but behind closed doors, he was someone entirely different. This type of behavior is often described as *covert narcissism*: charm and generosity in public, manipulation and emotional abuse in private.

I lost myself trying to become the woman he wanted me to be. I couldn't even wear skirts that touched my knees without being called names. He came home late, spent no time with me, and gaslighting became constant. I saw so many narcissistic traits. I tried to keep the marriage together, but I felt like I was drowning.

"The Lord is close to the brokenhearted and saves those who are crushed in spirit." —Psalm 34:18 "Love is patient, love is kind… it is not self-seeking, it is not easily angered, it keeps no record of wrongs." —1 Corinthians 13:4–5

A few months into our marriage, he told me he wanted to go to the Dominican Republic—with a friend. We hadn't even had a honeymoon. That request hit me like a wave of cold water. I had asked many times about taking a vacation together, about celebrating our union, and every time I was met with the same dismissive response: *"I can't take off from work."* Yet now, suddenly, he could take time off to travel with someone else?

He claimed to be the owner of his business, yet somehow, he couldn't make time for me. That contradiction cut deep. I realized then that he wanted to live like a single man while expecting me to play the role of a devoted wife.

If he wanted to act single, I was going to make his wish come true. I told him I wanted a divorce.

He didn't go on the trip—but he didn't stay to repair the damage either. He stayed home that week, sleeping all day, barely acknowledging me. I still came home from work to cook, clean, and tend to him. Even on holidays, when I longed for connection, he claimed he had to work.

It was in those moments—when I was giving everything and receiving nothing—that I began to see the truth. I was not his partner. I was his convenience. And I was done being invisible.

"Do two walk together unless they have agreed to do so?" —Amos 3:3 "You deserve someone who honors you, not someone who hides you." —Inspired by Proverbs 31:11

Later, I found out he had been living a double life—choosing to spend holidays with the other family he had always kept.

A few months before our anniversary, I suggested we visit his parents in St. Croix, hoping the change of scenery might help us reconnect. We stayed for two weeks and ended up catching COVID. But the real sickness in our relationship had already taken root.

When we returned, things didn't worsen because of the TV or his snoring. They worsened because I had already begun to emotionally check out. His actions had slowly chipped away at my trust, my affection, and my belief in the future we once imagined.

From the beginning, he insisted on sleeping with the TV on. I dismissed it to cater to him—just like I had dismissed so many other discomforts. But now, I saw it differently. Between the blaring screen and his relentless snoring, I wore earplugs and an eye mask just to get a few hours of sleep. He ignored me, spent hours scrolling TikTok, and intimacy became not just forced—but hollow and degrading.

By then, I had acquired more maturity. I could finally see the clown beneath the king costume. The illusion had faded, and what remained was a man who had never truly honored me—and a woman who had finally begun to honor herself.

"She is clothed with strength and dignity; she can laugh at the days to come." —Proverbs 31:25 "Forget the former things; do not dwell on the past. See, I am doing a new thing!" —Isaiah 43:18–19

One night, shortly after our return from St. Croix, I refused to lay my head on his chest. I told him I felt like nothing more than his maid, cook, and sexual object. He suggested we talk in the kitchen. But as usual, his voice grew louder, the gaslighting began, and I was blamed for everything.

When I walked away, I said, *"It takes two for an argument, and I'm not going to be the second one."* He followed me, demanding that I empty his suitcase. As I did, he attacked me—wrapping his arms tightly around me, pinning my arms and hands for what felt like an eternity. I screamed until he finally let go.

I fled the house in my pajamas—hysterical, afraid, and feeling completely unsafe in my own home. I went straight to my mother's.

"The Lord is a refuge for the oppressed, a stronghold in times of trouble." —Psalm 9:9

The next day, I discovered he had stolen jewelry and personal belongings. I called the police. They did nothing. Told me to wait until Monday to file a restraining order since it was Saturday. As for the stolen items, they said I'd have to request them back during divorce proceedings. I never recovered them—nearly $7,000 in belongings and money owed. Even with a prenuptial agreement stating the house was mine, the police said he could stay.

Thank God, he didn't.

That was the moment I realized: if I didn't speak up, no one would. If I didn't fight for myself, I might not survive the next time.

"Speak up for those who cannot speak for themselves… defend the rights of the poor and needy." —Proverbs 31:8–9

I filed for a restraining order. In court, the judge believed his lies, calling it a "bear hug." It was insulting—especially coming from a woman. Later, I learned he had a history of domestic violence. He had assaulted other women.

I also discovered that the mother of his children—whom he claimed was dying, frail, and bedridden—had actually been in remission for years. She wasn't dying. That story was just another manipulation tactic, designed to gain sympathy and silence my questions.

I learned she tolerated his involvement with other women because she benefited financially. That truth stung. But knowing what I now know about *Mr. Detour*—who he really was behind the charm and the lies—I can't help but wonder if she, too, was just another pawn in his game. Another woman caught in his web, surviving by playing along.

And yet… if she truly consented to the deception—if she knowingly stood by while he lied, manipulated, and emotionally destroyed other women—then that's not just sad. That's vile. That's disgusting. If she chose to be part of the performance, then they absolutely deserved each other.

I was never part of their act. I was the collateral damage.

But I survived.

And I will never again apologize for the fire I carry—for the anger that woke me up, for the pain that taught me discernment, and for the truth that finally set me free.

"Then you will know the truth, and the truth will set you free." —John 8:32 "The righteous cry out, and the Lord hears them; He delivers them from all their troubles." — Psalm 34:17

Even his children carried the weight of his deception. Whenever they visited my home, they were eerily quiet— too quiet for kids their age. They didn't laugh, didn't play, didn't ask questions. They didn't establish any rapport with me, as if they had been coached or conditioned not to speak. It felt unnatural. Robotic.

I remember looking into their eyes and seeing something I couldn't name at the time. Now I know—it was fear, confusion, and emotional suppression.

It was as if they had been brainwashed to protect his image, to never reveal what life was really like behind closed doors. And that broke my heart. Because children deserve safety, honesty, and love—not manipulation and silence.

I wasn't just witnessing the damage he caused in my life—I was seeing the ripple effect of his toxicity in theirs.

"Whoever causes one of these little ones to stumble, it would be better for him to have a millstone hung around his neck…" —Matthew 18:6

To anyone reading this who feels trapped, confused, or afraid: **Speak up. Don't wait. Call the police. Tell someone.** Your silence will not protect you. Your love cannot fix someone who is committed to breaking you.

Law enforcement failed me. The system failed me. But I will not fail myself again.

I am not just a survivor—I am a warrior. I got up. I stood tall. And I walked away with my dignity, my faith, and my voice intact.

"She is clothed with strength and dignity, and she laughs without fear of the future." —Proverbs 31:25

Looking back, I now understand that my worth was never meant to be measured by someone else's lies, manipulation, or broken promises. I had spent so much time trying to prove I was lovable, worthy, and enough—when in truth, I already was. I just hadn't seen it yet.

Every red flag I ignored became a lesson. Every tear I shed became proof that I was still standing. And every time I chose silence over confrontation, or endurance over self-respect, I was slowly drifting away from the woman God created me to be.

But even in that drifting, He never let go. He was guiding me—through the pain, through the confusion, through the unraveling—toward something deeper.

"The Lord will fight for you; you need only to be still." — Exodus 14:14 "He heals the brokenhearted and binds up their wounds." —Psalm 147:3

What did I learn?

Through this journey, I learned that my worth was never defined by someone else's lies, manipulation, or broken promises. It was mine all along—waiting to be reclaimed. I discovered that strength is born in the quiet moments when you refuse to settle for anything less than respect, honesty, and love. Every red flag I ignored became a lesson. Every tear I shed became proof that I was still standing. What I once believed was the end of my story turned out to be the beginning of my transformation. True freedom came when I reclaimed my voice, honored my boundaries, and chose myself—fully, unapologetically, and without hesitation.

🙏 Reflective Prayer

Deliverer and Protector,

Thank You for shielding me when I could not see the danger before me. Thank You for giving me the strength to walk away from lies, manipulation, and abuse, and for reminding me that my worth is not defined by anyone else's broken promises.

Lord, I confess that I ignored red flags and silenced my instincts, but You never abandoned me. Even in the darkest moments, You were my refuge. You turned what was meant to destroy me into lessons that now empower me.

Father, I ask You to continue healing the wounds of betrayal and restoring the places where fear once lived. Replace shame with dignity, sorrow with joy, and brokenness with wholeness. Teach me to honor my boundaries, to protect my peace, and to walk boldly in the freedom You have given me.

Your Word declares, *"So if the Son sets you free, you will be free indeed"* (*John 8:36*). I claim that freedom today. I choose to rise above manipulation, to embrace the truth of who I am in You, and to never again settle for less than respect, honesty, and love.

Thank You for transforming what I thought was the end of my story into the beginning of my new life. May my testimony remind others that strength is born when we choose ourselves, and that true freedom comes when we choose You.

In Jesus' name, **Amen.**

The Journey: When Peace Became My Priority

Like I mentioned before, the list could go on and on—the many different men we've encountered, the heartbreaks we've endured, the lessons we never asked for but desperately needed. But in the end, what truly matters isn't the men themselves.

It's the wisdom they left behind. The strength we discovered within ourselves. The clarity we gained through every experience.

Each chapter of pain became a stepping stone toward purpose. Each tear watered the seeds of resilience that now bloom in us.

"Weeping may endure for a night, but joy comes in the morning." —Psalm 30:5 "Consider it pure joy... whenever you face trials of many kinds, because you know that the testing of your faith produces perseverance." —James 1:2–3

During my marriage to *Mr. Detour*, I slowly began to lose sight of who I truly was. I wasn't living as my authentic self—I was shrinking, bending, and molding into the version of me he wanted. Not the woman I knew in my heart.

It's a painful thing to look in the mirror and not recognize the person staring back. Yet even in the exhaustion and confusion, I held on.

And today, I thank God for the self-worth and inner strength He planted deep within me—because those roots carried me through the storm.

"I praise You because I am fearfully and wonderfully made." —Psalm 139:14 "The Spirit of God has made me; the breath of the Almighty gives me life." —Job 33:4

That relationship taught me something I will never forget:

I am not anyone's maid. I am not anyone's emotional punching bag. I am not anyone's convenience.

I am a woman with dreams, responsibilities, and a divine calling. I deserve rest, respect, and reciprocity. And now I know—I do not have to settle for a life that drains me just to say I have someone.

"She is more precious than rubies; nothing you desire can compare with her." —Proverbs 3:15 "The Lord will fight for you; you need only to be still." —Exodus 14:14

What did I learn?

I learned that peace is priceless. That love should never cost me my identity. That saying "no more" isn't weakness—it's wisdom. That walking away isn't failure—it's freedom.

I don't want the same gift wrapped in different paper. I want something new. Something real. My happy ending.

But to get there, I had to stop searching for Mr. Right and start seeking God's will for my life. I had to ask myself the hard questions: Am I complete? What do I truly want? What are my deal breakers? Do I enjoy my own company?

Because the truth is, the journey doesn't begin with finding someone else, it begins with finding yourself.

As Matthew 6:33 reminds us: **"But seek first the kingdom of God and His righteousness, and all these things will be added to you."** I trust that as I walk in purpose, God is preparing someone who will walk beside me, not ahead of me, not behind me, but beside me. Someone who sees me, respects me, and values the woman I have become.

This chapter of my life isn't about bitterness, it's about clarity. It's about healing, growth, and reclaiming my joy. And yes, there are moments of loneliness and vulnerability, but I cling to His promises. **"And the peace of God, which surpasses all understanding, will guard your hearts and your minds in Christ Jesus."** (Philippians 4:7) That is the peace I finally regained—and no man is worth losing it again.

So, to any woman reading this who feels stuck, confused, or unsure—know this: You are not alone. Leaving a toxic relationship is not the end. It is the beginning of a new life. Your peace is worth protecting. Your voice matters. And your story is far from over.

You are allowed to want more. You are allowed to heal. And you are absolutely allowed to begin again.

When I first began writing this book, I imagined the final chapter would be my happy ending—a loving marriage, a story of earthly romance redeemed. I thought it would be about finding "the one." But God had other plans.

What He wanted to teach me wasn't about relying on a man—it was about learning to rely on Him. He wanted me to discover how to love myself first, to embrace singleness without shame, to set boundaries that honored my spirit, and to never settle for less than what I deserved: respect, trust, honesty, and love.

It wasn't about finding someone else. It was about finding me.

I had to understand my self-worth—not through the eyes of another, but through the eyes of God. I had to recognize that peace is not optional—it's sacred. That love should never cost me my identity. And that trusting Him with every step, even the painful ones, would lead me to something far greater than I had imagined.

What I once thought was the end of my story became the beginning of my transformation. I discovered that strength is born in the moments when you refuse to settle for less than you deserve. True freedom came when I reclaimed my voice, honored my boundaries, and chose myself—fully, unapologetically, and with God leading the way.

And through it all, I never gave up on love. As a reminder, I carry a tattoo on my forearm that reads *"L'amore trova una via"*—*Love finds a way.* It's more than ink. It's a declaration. A promise to myself that love, real love, will always find its way when you walk in truth, in healing, and in alignment with God.

As Proverbs 31:25 reminds us: **"She is clothed with strength and dignity; she can laugh at the days to come."**

That is the woman I've become. And that is the story God was writing all along.

🙏 Reflective Prayer

My Rock and Refuge,

Thank You for teaching me that peace is not a luxury—it is a necessity. A sacred gift from You that truly surpasses all understanding. There was a time I lost sight of who I was, shrinking myself to fit someone else's expectations, silencing my voice to keep the peace. But even in my exhaustion, You never let go. You planted strength in my spirit and whispered truth into my soul: I am Your daughter—worthy of love, respect, and joy.

Today, I choose to protect the peace You restored in me. I will no longer settle for relationships that drain me or compromise my identity. I will no longer confuse companionship with purpose. Instead, I will seek first Your kingdom, trusting that everything else will align according to Your will (Matthew 6:33).

Lord, help me to embrace the journey of self-discovery with courage. Teach me to ask the hard questions, to honor the boundaries You've helped me build, and to delight in the woman I've become. Remind me that healing is not weakness—it is strength. That clarity is not bitterness—it is freedom.

Your Word promises, "And the peace of God, which surpasses all understanding, will guard your hearts and your minds in Christ Jesus" (Philippians 4:7). I hold tightly to that promise. No man, no circumstance, and no storm is worth losing the peace You've given me.

Thank You for turning what I thought was the end into a new beginning. For transforming sorrow into joy, and brokenness into wholeness. Thank You for showing me that I never had to chase love to be worthy of it. That real love—Your love— finds a way.

May my story be a light for others. May it remind every woman that she is not alone. That her voice matters. That her peace is worth protecting. And that she is absolutely allowed to begin again.

In Jesus' name, **Amen.**

Afterword: From My Heart to Yours

Your peace is priceless. Your voice is sacred. And your story—no matter how messy or unfinished—is still being written.

I've come to believe that every heartbreak carries a divine lesson. That every detour, no matter how painful, might just be God's way of leading us back to ourselves.

A Needle in a Haystack is more than a collection of stories—it's my journey through love, betrayal, awakening, and healing. From "Mr. Wrong" to "Mr. Detour," I don't just expose the men I encountered—I reveal the strength I discovered, the wisdom I earned, and the peace I chose to protect.

This isn't a book about broken relationships. It's a book about transformation. About the sacred unraveling that happens when we stop chasing fairy tales and start embracing truth. About the courage it takes to choose ourselves, even when it hurts. About the grace that meets us when we finally let go.

Through every chapter, I've poured out my heart with honesty, humor, and faith. And if you've ever lost yourself in love, questioned your worth, or wondered if healing was possible—I wrote this for you.

🐟 Peace is not up for negotiation.

💔 Love should never cost you your identity.

🕊 Walking away isn't failure—it's the beginning of freedom.

Woven with scripture, prayer, and reflection, this book is my testimony—and I pray it becomes a lifeline for you. A reminder that you are not alone. That you are allowed to want more. That you are allowed to heal. And that you are absolutely allowed to begin again—with God leading every step.

Your story isn't over. It's just beginning. And this time, you get to write it with truth, grace, and power.

With love and purpose,

Kairy M. Springer

Kairy M. Springer

Glossary

Agape Love Unconditional, selfless, and spiritual love—most often associated with the divine love of God for humanity. It heals, forgives, and restores without expecting anything in return.

Purification The intentional process of emotional, spiritual, and mental cleansing in preparation for healing, growth, and new beginnings. Often involves solitude, reflection, and surrender.

Completeness A state of being whole and fulfilled within oneself—without relying on others to fill emotional or spiritual voids. True completeness is rooted in identity, not attachment.

Mr. Wrong A metaphor for unsuitable partners encountered on the journey toward discovering true love and divine alignment. Often familiar, yet misaligned with purpose.

Mr. Psycho A term describing emotionally unstable or manipulative individuals whose charm often masks deeper dysfunction. Their behavior can include gaslighting, control, and emotional volatility.

Mr. Cheap A person whose excessive frugality becomes inconsiderate and emotionally withholding in relationships. Often expects generosity without reciprocation.

Mr. Lazy Someone who lacks motivation, ambition, or follow-through—especially in the context of romantic partnership and shared responsibility. Their passivity drains momentum and hope.

Mr. Addiction A partner whose dependency on substances, habits, or destructive behaviors takes precedence over love, trust, and emotional safety. Their addiction becomes the third party in the relationship.

Mr. Gambler An individual who compulsively risks money or resources, often creating instability, secrecy, and emotional erosion in the relationship. Their addiction to risk undermines security.

Mr. Cheater Someone who violates trust and commitment through infidelity, dishonesty, or emotional betrayal. Their actions fracture intimacy and self-worth.

Mr. Detour A partner whose presence redirects your life away from peace, purpose, and authenticity. Often disguised as a blessing, but ultimately reveals itself as a lesson.

Covert Narcissist An individual who hides behind a mask of public charm and generosity, while privately manipulating, demeaning, and emotionally draining those closest to them. Their abuse is subtle but deeply damaging.

Gaslighting A psychological manipulation tactic where someone causes you to question your reality, memory, or perception. Often used to deflect responsibility and maintain control.

Emotional Suppression The act of silencing or minimizing one's feelings—either by choice or conditioning. Often seen in children or partners who have learned to protect others' reputations at the cost of their own voice.

Discernment The spiritual ability to perceive truth beyond appearances. A gift from God that helps us recognize red flags, hidden motives, and divine direction.

Red Flags Warning signs—often subtle at first—that indicate emotional, spiritual, or relational danger. Ignoring them often leads to deeper pain.

Self-Worth The recognition of one's inherent value, not based on others' treatment or approval, but rooted in God's design and love.

Boundaries Healthy limits set to protect emotional, spiritual, and physical well-being. Boundaries honor both self-respect and relational clarity.

Healing The process of restoring wholeness after emotional, spiritual, or physical injury. Healing is layered, sacred, and often nonlinear.

Resilience The ability to recover, adapt, and grow stronger after adversity. It's not just survival—it's transformation.

Spiritual Maturity The growth that comes from walking with God through trials, learning to trust His voice, and aligning your life with His truth.

References

Farlex. *"Mr. Wrong."* The Free Dictionary. http://www.thefreedictionary.com/Mr.+Wrong

Mary J. Blige & Drake. *"Mr. Wrong."* AZLyrics. http://www.azlyrics.com/lyrics/maryjblige/mrwrong.html

Britney Spears. *"Oops!... I Did It Again."* Genius Lyrics. https://genius.com/Britney-spears-oops-i-did-it-again-lyrics

Ed Sheeran. *"Thinking Out Loud."* Genius Lyrics. https://genius.com/Ed-sheeran-thinking-out-loud-lyrics

Biblical References

The Holy Bible. Various verses cited throughout the manuscript:

- **Amos** 3:3
- **Daniel** 9:9
- **Ecclesiastes** 3:1
- **Esther** 2:9, 2:12
- **Ephesians** 2:10, 5:11
- **Galatians** 6:7
- **Isaiah** 26:3
- **James** 1:2–3, 1:5
- **Jeremiah** 17:9

- **John** 3:16, 8:32, 16:13
- **Luke** 8:17, 22:42
- **Lamentations** 3:22–23, 3:23
- **Matthew** 6:14–15, 6:33, 6:34, 7:6
- **Nehemiah** 8:10
- **Philippians** 4:7, 4:11
- **Proverbs** 3:5–6, 4:23 (multiple), 12:22, 13:3, 13:12, 14:1, 14:12, 16:9, 26:11 (multiple), 31:11, 31:25
- **Psalm** 23:4, 30:5, 34:18 (multiple), 37:23, 46:10
- **Romans** 12:2
- **2 Corinthians** 6:14, 9:7, 12:9
- **2 Thessalonians** 3:10
- **2 Timothy** 3:16
- **1 Corinthians** 13:4–5, 15:33
- **Proverbs 31:11**

About the Author

I'm Kairy M. Springer—a woman shaped by trials, refined by grace, and anchored in faith. My journey has been anything but linear. From heartbreaks that shattered illusions to revelations that rebuilt my soul, I've learned that healing is not a destination—it's a decision. I write not from perfection, but from process. My words are born from tears, prayers, and the quiet strength of choosing peace over chaos.

A Needle in a Haystack is more than a book—it's a mirror, a ministry, and a map. It reflects the patterns I had to break, the truths I had to face, and the love I had to rediscover within myself. It's a testimony to every woman who has ever settled for less, questioned her worth, or lost herself in someone else's story. Through scripture, reflection, and raw honesty, I invite readers to reclaim their voice, protect their peace, and walk boldly into the purpose God designed for them.

I write for my daughters, for the women who feel unseen, and for the girl I used to be. My prayer is that these pages become a lifeline—a reminder that no detour is wasted when God holds the map.

Also About Kairy M. Springer

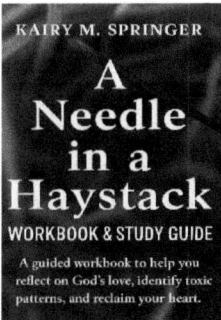

A Needle in a Haystack: Workbook & Study Guide

A Needle in a Haystack: Workbook & Study Guide is more than a companion to the book—it's a mirror, a ministry, and a map in motion. These pages are designed to guide you through the patterns I had to break, the truths I had to face, and the love I had to rediscover within myself.

This workbook is a testimony for every woman who has ever settled for less, doubted her worth, or lost herself in someone else's story. Through guided reflection, biblical insight, and raw honesty, I invite you to reclaim your voice, protect your peace, and walk boldly into the purpose God designed for you.

I created this guide for my daughters, for the women who feel invisible, and for the little girl I once was. My prayer is that each prompt becomes a lifeline—a sacred space to pause, reflect, and remember that no detour is in vain when God holds the map.

A Needle in a Haystack

www.ingramcontent.com/pod-product-compliance
Lightning Source LLC
Chambersburg PA
CBHW071145090426
42736CB00012B/2239